KEEP SMILING, STANDING STRONG

SE SCOTT

ISBN: 0984727302
ISBN 13: 9780984727308

CONTENTS

Thoughts on Poetry

POETRY is a noun. It means putting words, ideas, images, experiences, and people together. When the poet allows herself to open up, settle down, meet and collaborate with words, a poem may come through. There is so much fun in that if the poet plays around a little.

A POETRY ARTIST twists and turns words until the poem speaks and says, "Yeah! Now you're feeling what I mean. Let me tell more." This internalized conversation emerges as the poet writes the words. But like everything else in life; this takes a lot of time and testing to achieve.

MANY of my poems come out of experience. Usually, frustration with someone or something is the culprit. In that sense, frustration can lead to creating something positive like a poem. Poems can also emerge from strong feelings or passions. What does the poet feel passionately? Write a poem about it, and let the poem become an outlet for what is intensely felt. It's good therapy, too. As a teenager, I started writing about whatever I felt; writing became an enjoyable habit that kept growing and expanding. It's amazing how this happens.

ONCE I start writing I never know where I'll end up because writing is a moment by moment process. The poet must be willing to explore and change as she writes the words. Perhaps this is the key to understanding writing and the poem: always be a willing participant. Write on!

SE Scott

HIGH

LIGHTS

AND

SOCIALITES

The Lady That You Are

Sweet, you are
With the innocence of childhood
Trusting nature like a friend

You face foes you fear
You find love somewhere in bloom
You smile inside and spread light

"Try" is not a word you comprehend
"Building back up" is what you do
I cannot help admiring the lady inside of you

You learned the hard way
And expected "them" to understand
They may never know this woman who is to me so grand

Your eyes say, "sit and stay a while"
Your story you so beautifully unfold
My ears are like butterflies, Lady
Settling upon a wonder filled power tale

You can tell me repeatedly
While others search the wide world through
There will never be one so lovely, clean, or clever
As the lady I found in you!

✡ ✡ ✡

AIN'T I A WOMAN?
AM I NOT A PEARL?

They call me a ho' and say I'm dumb.
They identify me based on where I'm from.

But, ain't I a woman
Am I not a pearl

Some think I'm kinda cute, others say I'm too thin.
They look at my hair, my face, the color of my skin.

But look beyond that, 'cause that's not where I end.
I'm true to life. I don't have to front or pretend.

Ain't I a Woman?
Am I Not a Pearl?
I been turned out and in tryin' to understand how to be,
You see, I want to bring a smile to my family

Am I not a pearl?

Thirteen years gone. I'm growing up too fast.
I'm lookin' and wonderin' which friends are gonna last.
We have to face double-faced dragons that hide, hide from the light.
It's too bright, another day brings—a brand new fight.

Pull back the screen, and look—I mean, what happens to
     those beautiful pearls?

✳ ✳ ✳

Those Who Seek

Those who seek to bring you down with damaging words untrue
With killing stares or lies that glare
With everything they do

Are pitiable people who lost their way pray for them, will you?

Those who seek to stop your start hold so much turmoil inside
Before they happen to rot away
Get on your knees and pray

Those who seek to give their grief may keep on giving with no relief
You keep smiling, standing strong
You keep smiling, standing strong

You keep smiling, keep standing strong pray for those who wish you wrong

✡ ✡ ✡

SAY SOMETHING

To be young shy or demure
To say very little or be unsure
Speaking is a challenge
"Too quiet" is a name
When others look
You may feel awful shame
I know the feeling
There
Isolation wondering
Avoiding the stare

When I started teaching
My students were the same
No talking youngsters, I remembered the pain
Not knowing what to say when the time came
"Say something", I told them
"You have a voice. Talk out your shyness
Make a choice.
Push! Push!" I urged them again
Soon they talked. Many words came

If you are shy, or struggle opening up
Say something, hear your voice
It is pleasant and pleasurable too
The choice is yours
Let the world hear you

✡ ✡ ✡

Some Search the Wide World Through

Let me tell you about Mother; listen and you will learn
About a woman who is sweet no matter which way I turn

It's not easy raising me when I don't understand what I do
Or when I speak before I think, thoughts fully through

Sometimes I wonder about her, how kind she is and why
She stands with me facing foes; she'll fight for me, no lie.

She tolerates me like crazy; she trusts me like a friend
She puts up with me being lazy; she is strict--but still bends.

My mother has eyes that talk; I know her stories well
My ears listen like butterflies to the stories she loves to tell.

She had to try harder when it was very hard to try
Mother keeps on forward; her goals she would never deny

Love is in bloom somewhere; I feel it inside, close
She cares so much for me; I lift her up a toast

Mother, tell me again; some search the wide world through
And never find a lady like the one I found in you.

✫ ✫ ✫

Extensions

Inside the framed borders on the wall
A woman I see
Clothed so purely gently
Holds me head to breast
Loves me
In time, thoughts
Light soft eyes, arms hug

We kiss when we meet
Outside
Feels so fine, we dine
An easy glass of sweet wine
We toast
Bon appetit!

I love to hear her talk
Vous parler bien
We walk watching others pass
Lincoln Center, museums, botanic gardens
Other dreamy delights
Exhaust our days
Imagination and its peculiar ways
Far away from home, sweet rest
No distance between our jests
Au revoir!

She still loves me
That is all I see
No borders or colors prime
No manicured angle or smooth pastel

She is real and divine
That treasured embrace helps me unwind,
She draws me in, I draw no lines
Inside her painted view

✧ ✧ ✧

THAT IS HOW YOU ARE

a heart big enough to fill the sky
a love deep enough to not ask why
devotion strong enough to never part
faith long enough than any map can chart
mercy good enough to repeat again
salvation sure enough to erase any sin
a friend close enough no wall could ever bar
a spirit sweet enough…that is how You are.

✿ ✿ ✿

REDBIRD

Thanks for resting in the grape bush,
I spied you, once, in a tree
Winter's here, brown is all mingled
With ice and snow

Your royal redness this morning
Delights my heart, I smile
In places secret and unknown

This social call, this desolate day
Broadcasts your travel your flitting way
Cart your joy; I concede
You are the gift; I humbly heed

✿ ✿ ✿

TAKE
TWO

SUBSTITUTION

It was cool and it was sweet
It soothed bubbling waters crouching deep
It satisfied and abated time
It gave shimmering joy and tasted divine

In that moment, my mind did embrace
Emotions pressing nary morsel to waste
The pleasure I craved
Some unknown good
The taste of a dream, I dreamed as I could
Until it was over, I relished every drop
Wishing to go on, I had to stop

But I think, I'll think about it again
Until the day substitution ends

✫ ✫ ✫

I'm Not a Fan

I'm not a fan scanning faces in "Hollywood"
Or on a rush for that air-brushed artistic look
You have changed yourself over
For branded style
You can't hook me on a line, online,
Though you have a line everyday
Hey!
I can't read for seeing you
The twitter tosses, the interview
Can't hold me like glue
You're not so hot in my hand,
I have Church-Beat Radio on demand

Wait!
I remember how
You liked Spades in college, yo'
Joker was wild, high and low
We talked real good then
About what would happen
When glory came our way
But that was back "in the day"
Dreaming truth, nothing fake
Now, it's all you.
Highlight your name
Just another celebrity in love with fame

What's the use in made-up lies?
You still get paid as another child dies
There in the crux, the bolts and nuts
Of spectacular color you supply
Make that money, lose your soul
It's not your image I behold
Use to love that thing you lost

Down in your heart
So beautiful, so boss
I knew about that but I see this
I felt you there what went amiss
Whatever, whatever, I 'm not a fan

✧ ✧ ✧

I Just Want to Tell You

I just want to tell you who you think you fooling
Walking inside like you think you rulin'
Yeah, you lookin' good outside, but inside it's cold

What is that stone, Peter was a rock
Don't deny my Jesus you might be shocked
He's coming back again but your heart ain't right
He's coming back again like a thief in the night

I just want to tell you who you think you fooling
Walking inside like you think you rulin'
Yeah, you lookin' good outside, but inside it's cold

On TV doing reality, is that what you think He called you to be
A movie star--Oh, you like a reel; stars in your eyes.
How does it make you feel?

I just want to tell you who you think you fooling
Walking inside like you think you rulin'
Yeah, you lookin' good outside, but inside it's cold, it's cold

I heard you were searching for a love you never found
If you got an issue Jesus is in town
He's calling you out, what is the deal
He can show you how to live a life that's real

Open your mouth; let Him hear you say
Father, I give my life to you, today

I just want to tell you
I just want to tell you
I just want to tell you
I'm glad you made it through

I just want to tell you
I just want to tell you
I just want to tell you
God bless you

✼ ✼ ✼

THE CONFESSION

I have seen that look a hundred times
that face of shame, embarrassment reminds
me of other mouths reading lines
confessing crimes
of infidelity

Narrate your story apologize
Show us how you put on disguise
While your family faces
a barrage of lies drip nervously
from your mouth

"My family and friends did not deserve
my scandalous behavior which has occurred
Turn your cameras from them
and see that in the dark,
 it was all about me"

"I am so sorry, I apologize
Did I say sorry, didn't mean to surprise
Sorry again for the host of lies
Do forgive me, do not despise
my lousy excuses, my alibis"

✻ ✻ ✻

EARTH AND SAND

I look like the earth; my sister resembles sand
She often likes to challenge me about where I stand
She says that I am ignorant, and claims that I am fooled
She says that my belief in Jesus is intellect unschooled
She does not see the picture I get by reading His word
Our relationship is personal. He lifts me up; I surge
I toss those words from others
From those who misunderstand
Do you know of His intimacy?
Have you ever held His hand?
He is a spirit so sweet, forever present within
Mover of layered mountains, dogmas that smother and spin

Creator of the earth; architect of the sand
Look to my sister; help her understand.

✵ ✵ ✵

BUILT TO LAST

Old and gray is beauty
Time caused her to fade
Botox and creams, highlights and dreams
Could not defeat the old maid
It's kind of sad to think
Her loveliness doomed to shrink

Body beautiful, fit and spry
Works to perfection in youth
So high, but age which holds the upper hand
Tugs at what was once grand
Declining years give way
To rigid journeys of decay

To build a life, to run and run
To spread some seed, to catch the sun
A family grows resembling you
Their guiding light to see them through
To hear the world, it calls so loud
Temptations pull you with the crowd

What to do you often ask
In your weakness you dare not bask
It happens once upon a day
In the moment along the way
You are flesh and like the grass
Only eternal was built to last

What is eternal?
Lily fields, no not so
Who is eternal?
One who kneels
Understand this temporal cast
The skin you are in, not built to last

✡ ✡ ✡

SINCERITY

Like a leaf swaying from side to side flowingly falls
Withered and brown from life
I was lost and wanted to fold head first into chest
Into abdomen, thighs into legs
Feet airtight seals

I was a leaflet, so distant from a place within my soul
My destination, unknown
A solar system, a yolk less mess moving
I was nowhere, matter floating like balloons
Scouring the sky

I heard the molder say
Let me show you--you
No summary, synopsis, or outline will do
My mistakes, stupid mindless acts I saw
A stale scent there on the floor
Purple, orange, and blue stink
I knew it would not be pretty
But then the molder said
Come, I still want you
He was so kind
I cried in His arms
He kissed my forehead
Imagine that
I was at my worse and He embraced me
He favored me, sincerity

I never thought I could be so loved or wanted
What can I give you in return
The molder said your heart
My heart I gladly gave
He became an exquisite treasure

And I became his beloved

✧ ✧ ✧

Exponential Curve

Greater than a four square curve
He gives us more than we could ever deserve
Yield not to temptation, it is He we serve
The Spirit within is the voice we heard

Commitment is all
He has my heart because in innocence He died
Show some gratitude He passed the test
He was tried. Give all to Him and abide,
The exponential curve has arrived

Faith is the key
God has proved; trust in His son,
See how He moves,

Remember that walk on water; Peter did go, our Savior let him
So He could show, it is all possible if we only believe
Lean on His shoulder, to His hand cleave

That exponential curve, it will be there to serve
It is that all powerful spirit within
God's Holy Ghost, and the word

✵ ✵ ✵

He Came to Make Us Whole

From the beginning of time
He had us in mind
The mission decided
The steps planned
The child was born
And grew to a man
He was beloved
By our Father so pure
He stood in his destiny
He lived to ensure

We come back to our Father
As sinless and free
When we give our hearts
And make this plea:

Lord, here I am! I pray you will forgive
Sin in my life, in my heart live
I believe you are the Christ, God's treasured gold
Save me now and make me whole
Amen

✧ ✧ ✧

EMAIL EXCHANGE

Sender

But we do have a same "blood"
Connection
When this is all over
You will see that
We are closer than
You ever thought
Deep!

Revelation

Receiver

Whoa,
You are right,
You are just too
Deep for me!
I know our blood connection.
Christ, the Lord!
I am so excited right now…
Thanks for the reminder

✳ ✳ ✳

TEST IF I

This is not just poetry
It's preaching here
With faith in God that I'm reaching a dear
Lost soul in dire need
Not only with words
But with word that feeds

Will you please listen as His Spirit speaks in you?
He is the friend that you never knew
And His arms are stretched out too
Most intimately, He knows you so see
The depth of His heart, His ability
Jesus is the only one who can set free

One day I heard Him call me too.
Busy, so busy I was doing my thing
Until I fell down and felt the sting
Of life kicking me again
That was when I cried out His name
Embraced His love; never was the same

I learned the truth, that God is real
In Him salvation, I was humbled and healed
This life, this truth and recompense
Is why I served Him from that day since
Take your step, He waits for you
Confess with your mouth, see what He can do!

✧ ✧ ✧

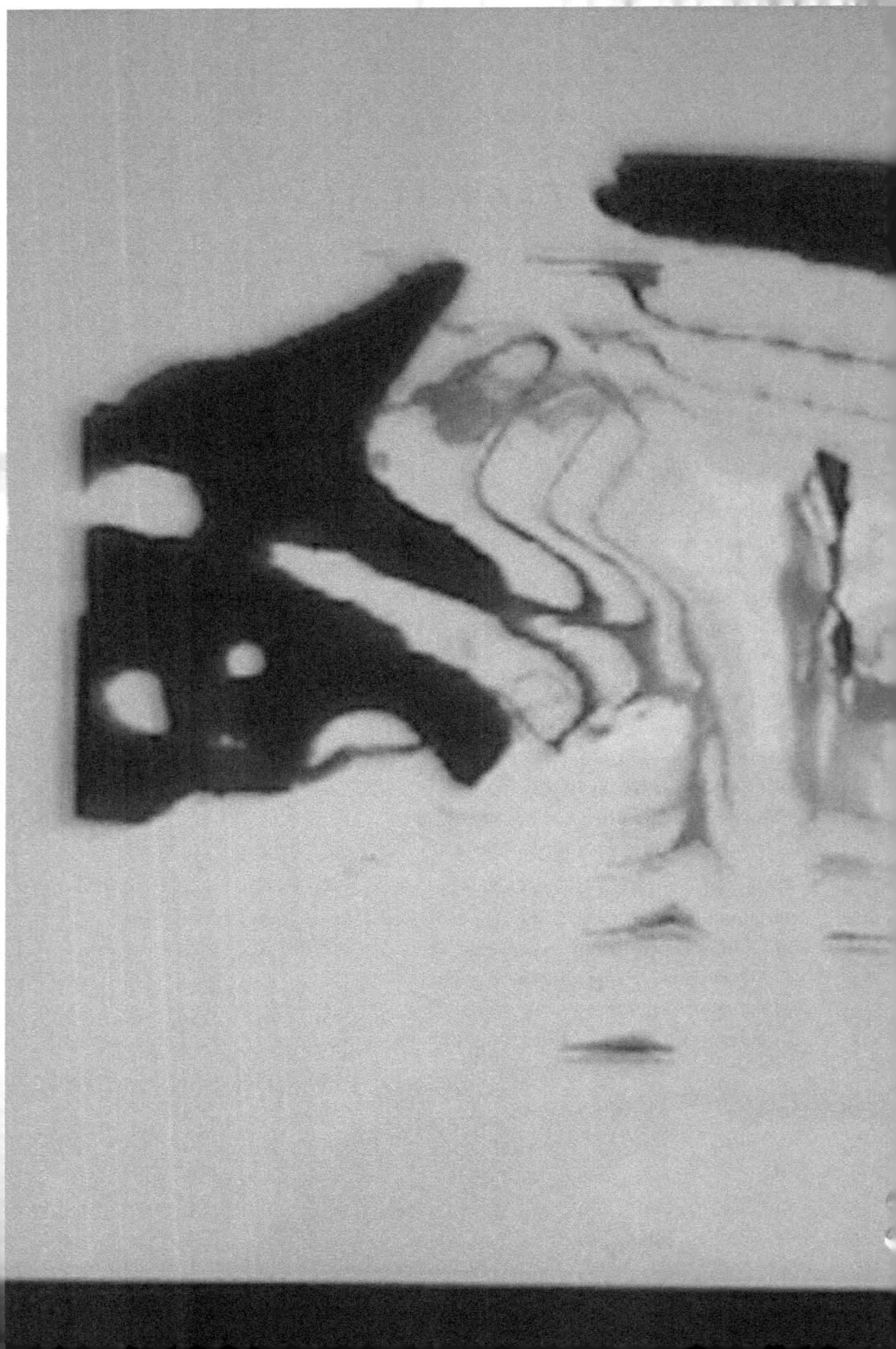

FRAGMENTS

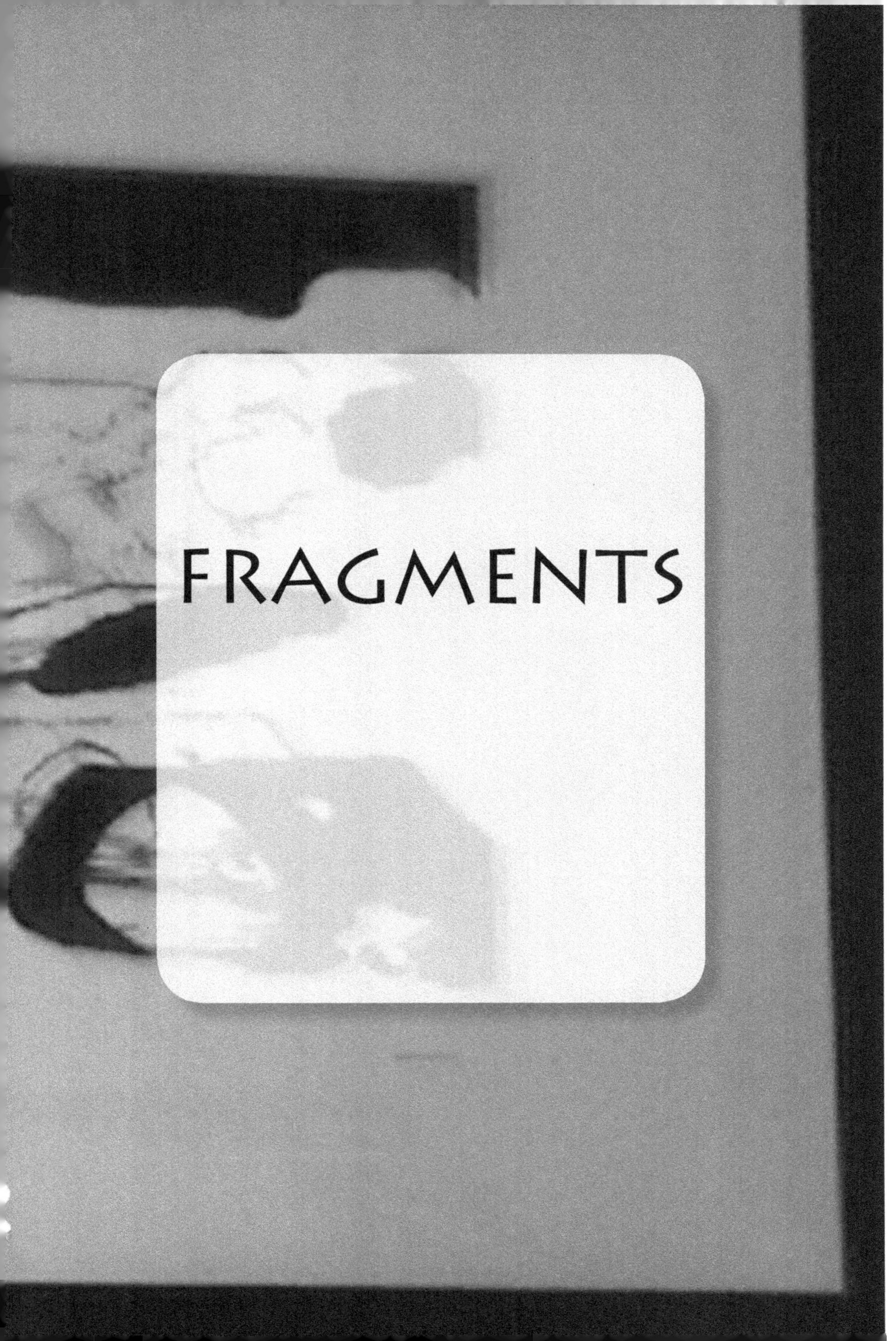

THIS RIFT

Is this rift about the pain you felt for days emerging, again?
While I stand stranded and dry
There is tension
It sends me into a zone
Where emotions fly
Like the time my mother died
Or a lover went away

All those years moving back into corners, hurting
Life, it is heavy, sometimes

Will this rift make us die?
We were friends, was that a lie
Is it time for us to quit
Feelings are so strong; they reign tight
All this nothingness that doesn't act right

I cannot talk anymore
But is it true, does time heal wounds
Just step away, don't call to soon
Disappointment still lives in my house
Hurt plays cat and mouse
I will talk about you in a general way
As a person of the past
No more to say,
Moving on

✫ ✫ ✫

SELF-TALK

Sincerely
I am bare today
See echoes of this searching self
Burn within
Pull back the screen that flips, twists for you
Reveal steep hole, deep layers of moldy secrets
And things

Is anybody home?
A house, a Volvo, a test tube baby
Make me face the dragons that hide
A failed marriage hear lies
Pull back the screen
Truly,
I am bare

Must we go among the low rocks?
Must we tarnish our clean good intentions with dust and doubts?
Must we part ways?

The air is fresh when I think of you
Why don't you mirror me true?
You leave instead
So, I sanction myself gently
As antagonistic forces stand, point
Dog me, dogging me

I hold the truth
Self-evident
We part ways
No longer yours, endlessly
I am bare

Pardon me, while I

While I shield myself
While I shift to a place
Of genuine height

✼ ✼ ✼

DREAMS FOR BETTER DAYS

Thunder clouds move overhead as passing time makes me feel
So out of touch
Like some insignificant mountain subdued by ancient snow
Yesterday, I was young
Today, I am silent like the mountain

Where is the spring air that buds within?
Can these dry bones live?
Sweltering palms question my unseasoned self
Perspiration lingers, then falls

Life is full but timing is everything
It is not cordial.
Slow stagnant feet trip over
Dreams for better days

Oh, the falling leaves! How beautiful they are.
A soft breeze ushers thin iron strands up and down
My head, the wind curls, and these eyes witness
The stalling corners, blink, blink, and blink back years

Visions I see, a crystal oasis of winter wonderlands
Pushed away boxes buried
A graveyard of silent dreams
Decayed, horrible, and undone

✶ ✶ ✶

Holy Ground

This is the place where I am standing
It is a promise, a solid rock

This is where I stand
I won't run or walk away

This is the place where I leave the past behind
I am renewed, and one of a kind

This is the place where I stand
My bold light lifted high and free

This is the place. Yes, it is!
Where I stand is holy ground

✲ ✲ ✲

OUT OF MY
HEART FOR 911

First, it was what I heard that made me sick
Then what I saw...saw
Dust, fire, emotions and steel tearing, debris
Stealing tears, swollen fears, and life jerked into death
In the seconds, moments, and hours of a nightmare
But it was day, a good morning gone berserk
Above the blue sky, a world was torn beneath us
Exposing shock, and grotesque pain
Dirt, faces, bodies, cries and last goodbyes
Eyes watering sorrows, heads shaking, aching
And breath-making the world numb

When the first rain came purifying the site
A little comfort came too. Time made an uneasy turn
A little less pain but a flood, an avalanche
Of stories, of heroes, of survival, of hope
We will get through this, yes we will
Pulling and tugging, holding and hugging
Humanity's mouth brought many like me
To bow and pray with empathy
The horror of it all paved a circle of sympathy

When the second rain came emotions flared once more
It was a time, deep in the night when peace was vulnerable in rain,
I think God could not hold back His tears
And I understand, for I too cried
As the awful stench told of truth in a dreadful way
Wails riding horses, varied voices riding nocturnal winds
Rousing me up, membrane and spirit, heavy heart set sail
It was dark; I felt queasy; uneasy tender drops

I thought of each life that ended that way
Within my soul there in the night I sang
A song of lament for the lives lost, and pain it cost
On that mournful September day

✫ ✫ ✫

THREADS

One scenic path leads to a narrow trail of sparsely spread
      trees looming high above

A secluded creek below a long tedious hill

The picnic house on a sunny day provides a temperamental view
      of the lake in the distance
on the other side of Prospect Park Brooklyn

There is a solemn spot in Juneau where cool snow-capped mountains
Surround a glacial lake
Where an almost inaudible drip gently subdues the pervasive silence
Humbly, I approach
Listening for ancient secrets of totemic peoples
And leaving a bit more humane

Concealed within the tunnel of private thoughts terror and one dark day
The guilt, shame no longer remain dead spirits cannot be stilled

Let my eyes be pleasantly pleased
Sultry and flamboyant, sweetheart, you
Cheer me in springtime, draped
Colors like a tropical fruit
My nostrils eagerly delight in
Intoxicating fragrance
Inhale, slow, deep breath
Euphoria!

Light, airy
Dopey dunce
Dear Hibiscus flower
Will I ever rise?

✫ ✫ ✫

LAST MOTHER'S DAY

I did not know that was your last mother's day
Your final walk on solid ground

I distanced you in my youth, loved you years since then
That spirited light glistens in no other eye

Time moved you away from me
 Holidays are like history lessons among family and friends

But, I cannot touch you
Do you see me here, nursing deep wounds?

What do you say?

Go on
Be grateful
I am still

✪ ✪ ✪

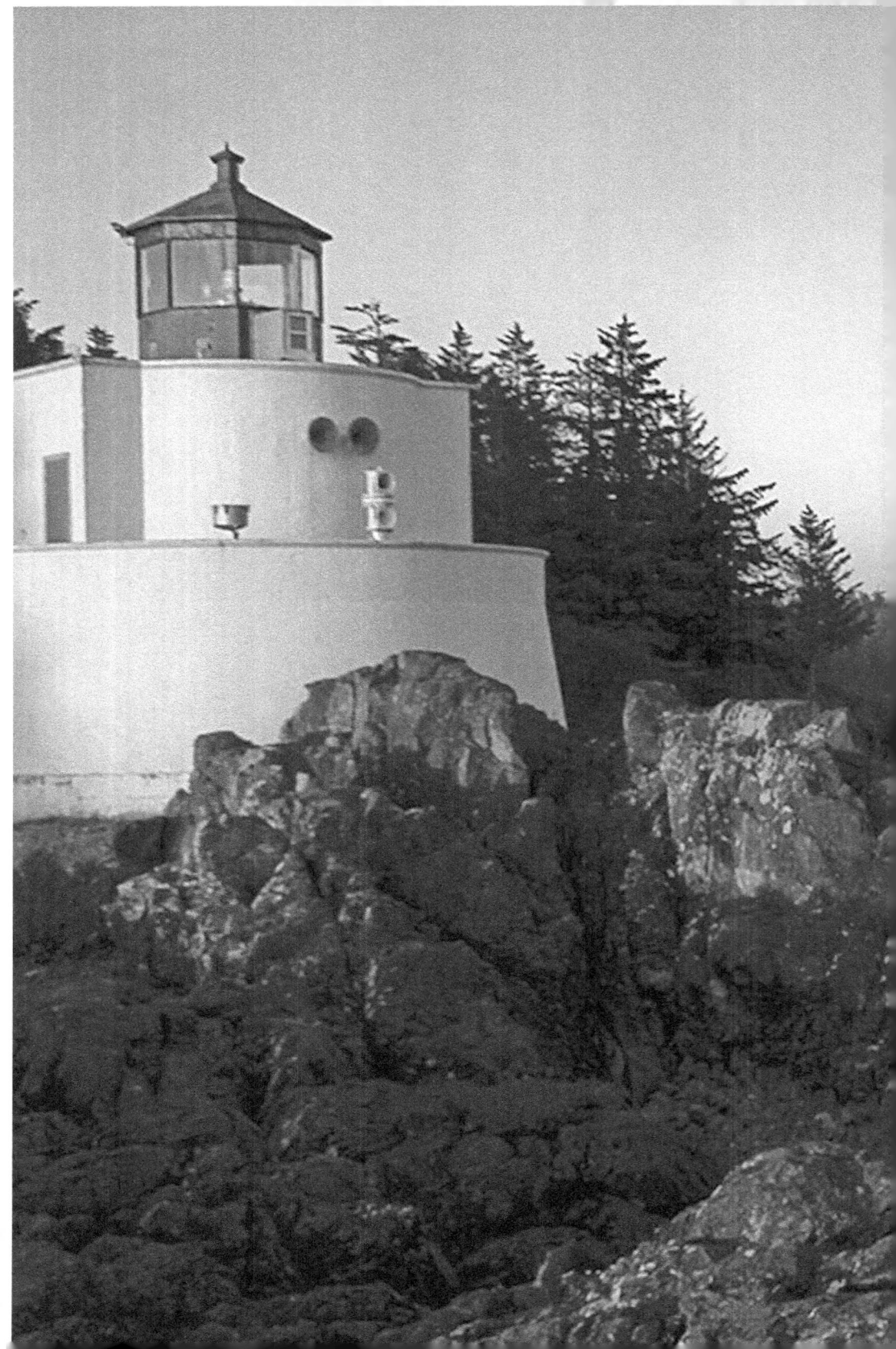

The Happy Place

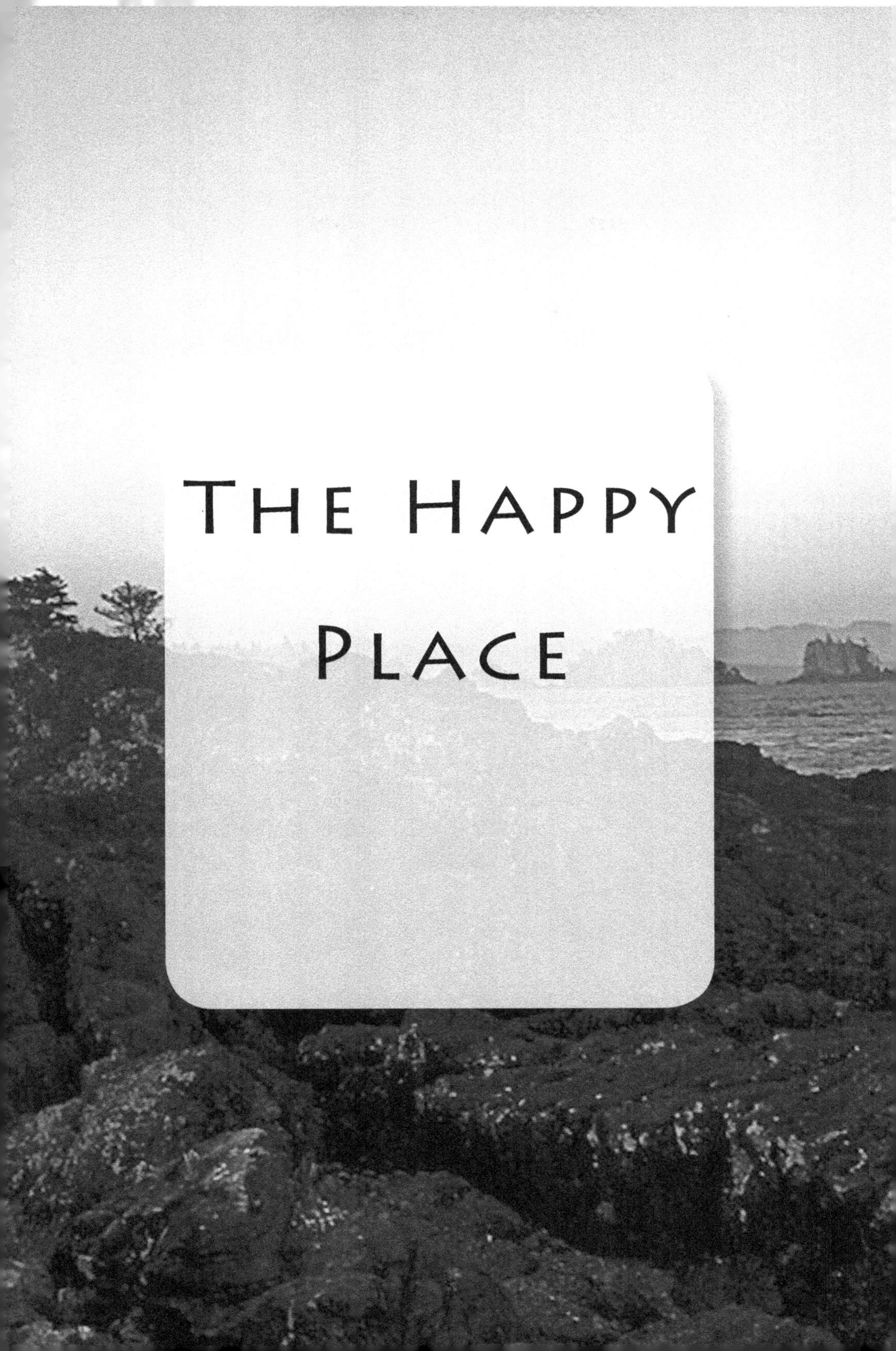

Utopian by the Sea

Every island is a sea island copper-toned in tan
With arms opened wide on vacations, I stride
To an island by the sea

Every island does empower me to dwell in coral by the sea

Mother comes from a sea island,
A Gullah beauty is she; her smile is lasting.
Her voice soft as angels' wings
She is an angel to me

Father's word made this island stretch long along coastal sands.
Isn't that grand! Geechee, Gullah, and me
Splash one another, so freely.
A noble, gentle man is he who holds a pedestal for family.

Every island is a sea island; we are vibrant fresh air fun
Whether beaching or dining, reading or sand designing
We are utopian by the sea.

✿ ✿ ✿

THE INVITATION

L. A.
P. A.
Italy
You like to travel
Just say the word, the word
I saw you walking down the street one day
Hey hey, looking good

When was that you say
You like to travel
Going my way
Just say the word, the word
Run run blue sky
Kiss, tears, goodbye
Here we go, again name a date say when

Heard a song about you
Melody through and through
You knew my name
You saw me when I came
I was hidden kinda shy
You held me in your eye
I wondered by and by

Just say the word, the word
You see through me
Wanna fly like bumblebees
I am just so
Enamored by you
Say the word, the word
I like to travel

✺ ✺ ✺

A Day in the Life

My dear mother is gone away
She said she would be back
Later today

My dear father is working hard
In the boss's lumber yard

My two brothers gone to play
"You can't come!"
They always say

Here I am about to cry
Everybody's gone, why can't I?

✡ ✡ ✡

I Didn't Stay There

In the days when I was a child life was so simple
Growing up was a wish, a hope to be
My own person without the poverty
But I didn't stay there

Teenage years were trying times
Sexual advances, temptations and crimes
Inner city woes made me aspire
To have higher goals than a boy friend
Poverty was still nipping my feet
Love peered around corners rather curiously
I eyed a few of interest to meet
But I didn't stay there

Along and along the diploma finally came
It was wonderful hearing my name
A teacher once said to me, you are the future
Now I see how purpose takes place
And to what degree
I liked and I loved, I dismissed and found
One to marry at a time that seemed sound
But I didn't stay there

A strange land I visited, a place I had never known
Took time to reflect, to see how I had grown
I noted the losses, and counted the gains
But I didn't stay there

People like things came through a revolving door
But none had the power they had before
No strength to take what I refused to give
No words to recite the way I should live
I listened to follow what I heard within me

Ignored the naysayers of negativity
I didn't stay there

I learned to consume the consumers of me
Wisdom took back authority
Refuted every rival, this canvas I claimed
I didn't stay there, and I remain

✡ ✡ ✡

Will He Come Reading Poetry

Will he come reading poetry in the wide open plains?
Will he be on television tenderly calling my name?
Is he on the east coast or from the international world?
Wherever he is; I am his girl!

He probably is younger than I
As long as he is cute, in shape
I want a Christian man for a mate
To body build me a house on a hill

It does matter; he's got to be my dream fulfilled

Will he like children, if not, he is bland
I will send him back, not my kind of man
A workaholic interests me no more,
Is he true and has integrity in his core?

These would be the reasons I am attracted to him
Falling hard in love because he goes to the gym!

✲ ✲ ✲

I Have a Man

A gentleman said to me one day,
"No woman can be on the streets without a man!"

And I replied, "I have a man. In fact, I have three."
His face was rich with curiosity.

Silence listened; my mouth, his ear
It was a mystery to him so queer

"The one who is Father to a sacrificed son,
The third is spirit of the Holiest one.

Three entities wrapped to me
I am not alone; don't believe what you see."

The gentleman had no more to say.

✡ ✡ ✡

A SONG FOR SURE

I did. I did. I did not know.
I had ideas for a song show
Certain. So sure I did want to be.
I travelled. I thought. I let my mind free.

Along the path I passed many friends
A smile, a lie, some wearing grins.
The rift, the drama, the spoken word spins
I moved the stage lift to far end

I see, the sea, a cultural tour
What is life a song for sure
Bread and wine a star sublime
Sometimes I feel the universe chime.

The world--it picks, it plucks me bare
My purpose it sits as still as a chair
The trail I travel should lead somewhere
I saw a rainbow arched in my hair

"Poor soul lost, still standing there
Blinded by sights, heavy sun glare
Wanted so much to be on your own
Come, my child, not fully grown!"

Back, I hurried with focused speed
My mind did race like new breed
I know. I know. I know the song now
but how to mend this rift with brown cow?

The song is cute. It speaks of peace
mountains, valleys, sky, and peaks
It gives strength for each day
Nurture, love tracks through the fray.

Time to hit the mark really straight
Sing on purpose a love refrain
No minute to spare
Before He calls my name

✤ ✤ ✤

FIRST LOVE

GOD IS TRUE

It came in a prayer that went like this
Through thick and thin He has been
Our refuge, our strength
The Lord was there when we could care
Less about His love, so precious so rare

Once so wasted by this crazy world
We followed what we hardly knew
Until one day, we discovered His way
And found
Our God is true

✧ ✧ ✧

AFFIRMATION

The child in me does yield
Wholeheartedly towards you
I wish to be high on spiritual things
Oh, good God, build me
To stand for what is true
I wish to be a field that buds
Genuine love

✫ ✫ ✫

IN HIS REALM

The answer, the solution, it is He
Alpha and omega meshed into three

The aches, the worries; that ails you and me
He beckons us come! Oh, taste and see

He is good, solid and sound
All that we need can surely be found

In the God of David, the one Goliath did not know
Until an encounter with a stone's throw

David conquered that Philistine, a fearsome foe
When the God of Abraham Himself did show

Today, in our most pressing needs
God can bring us out if we follow His lead

Whatever giant, mountain, or flood
Cannot triumph we are covered by His blood

It is true, no challenge can overwhelm
He protects his own; we live in His realm

✷ ✷ ✷

ON THE RUN

I thought I had everything
I needed for the road
Double checked oversights
Went through all the codes

Off I went, independently and free
Couldn't tell me anything
I was Queen Bee
Found a destination. Look at me!

In the meantime, that unknown in between time
Something I certainly needed
Was mistakenly left behind
I assumed I was rich, but how poor how blind

I didn't realize the greatness of the flaw
until I grabbed my things
Horror is what I saw
or wished I did not see

How could this be
I recounted my steps
Named them one by one
Reviewing all aspects, I still was not done

It was a slight second
I was caught on the run
My mind was far away
"You can't undo what's done"

 Assessing the situation
gave a little ease
a moment of preoccupation
thawed me from that freeze

Onward I went anyway
with the business I intended
Here and there a thought came
trying to be long-winded

Experience is a teacher
torture not a friend
"She didn't give in to pressure
but went until the end"

Over the roads I travelled back from where I had been
I thought about His goodness and went further within
I prayed a prayer to the Father
To Him I humbly came

I asked Him for the mercy
He gives in Jesus' name
I know that He is able to make wrong things right
I place cares in His hand; He is a guiding light

Trust is a requirement
He asks for little more
My purse was sitting peacefully
when I opened up the door.

✡ ✡ ✡

HE KNOWS

He knows what it is like in a desperate state
Madly alone without a helping mate
Rejected, unreachable, by love anywhere
Ignored by others, disregarded of care

He knows what it is like--the Son of God
He walked your way once when it was hard
It was painful on His way to that cross
He was forsaken, and like garbage tossed

Life is a cascade of shadows that endlessly pound
Us with blows and like dust we settle on a mound

He knew what it is like, He laid his life down
But be of good cheer, He now wears a crown
In glory He reigns
In Him be free
He rose from a life for our victory
Our precious redeemer, He knows our state
Give Him your destiny,
He knows your fate

✫ ✫ ✫

WORD

Oh Lord,
Your word is beautiful
It touches me so powerfully

It lightens the way
Gives faith for a better day
It renews and holds steadily

Your goodness, I see
Giving hands
Loving me

✵ ✵ ✵

ALL ELSE SUBSIDES

I am only a foreigner here; I did not come to stay
A little while this path will be no more
Soon I will walk through another door
I am not sad nor wear a frown
And do not hesitate to lay this world down

Each day He gives; I aim to live
Abundantly and free
Not in a corner, nor by the side
Of some unpublished road

For all He gave, I can be brave
Wear a smile for this short while
No accumulation, no mansion, no child
Yet life is grand
Inside me, He stands

His word abides
With me, all else subsides

✾ ✾ ✾

ANOTHER INSPIRATION

In my ears the words did come
Tumbling to me through a hum
In my eyes, I could see
A miracle birth in front of me
Another inspiration I heard you brought
Through your servant a message I caught
In the song, in the dance, in the art
I had a chance
Once again to acknowledge you
Our one true guide beaming through

You may use any open heart for your purpose to impart
Another inspiration

✧ ✧ ✧

Keep on Song

Moments of despair left sadness in my heart
Dreams tumbled quickly, I fell apart
With nowhere to go, no company to seek
My head bent in lowliness, my eyes did weep
Then deep in the spirit, far beyond the ear
A soft-spoken whisper, a song I could hear.
It was an old song

"Ain't gonna let nobody turn me around
Turn me around, turn me around"

The kind of song my mother's mother might sing

"got to keep on walkin', walkin' up the King's highway"

Gentle words, they were soft and sweet, unraveled in my ear
a message to keep.
Forceful words, I couldn't help but see. Somebody was singing,
especially for me.

"Keep on walkin', walkin' up the king's highway"

Up I sat, listening hard to confirm; instruction I heard
the comfort I yearned.

"Down is not out, be courageous and bend
yourself towards faith, try again"

This song untangled that winding snare; it testified of hope
in a hopeless nowhere.
I lit up, like a candle light
My head aimed forward pulling strength and might.

✲ ✲ ✲

MOST VALUABLE PLAYER

When He labeled me MVP I said, "Oh Lord, not me!
I have little to offer, don't you see!"
That tag was one too hard to face
I did not commit; I shunned being an ace.

After some time, I began to feel strange
What was missing, my hilt, my range?
I realized the "regular" left me feeling poor
I looked at myself, and wanted much more.

MVP, can I rise to the name
Can I make a difference without lusting fame?
I do have longings; I know you hold the list
Of "works to do" yet fear persists.

Father, clear my heart of the issues it holds
Sever each one until your spirit unfolds
Destroy the old, define the new
Let MVP be my motivating cue.

Stepping out of struggle, ready to contend
I am that "Hail Warrior" You wanted to send
I understand now, your place for me
I desire that label, MVP.

✵ ✵ ✵

SCRIPTING WORDS

My mind says to me that it does not see
how I could be
 MVP
Thoughts do not rule destiny
Just because it mentally flows
doesn't make it true
Or how it goes

I am not my mind; I am higher than that
Truth stands stronger than the chitter chat

MVP is appropriately the exact image
 I was made to be

✧ ✧ ✧

Dare
To Be

SCALING THE WALLS

Take to the ocean where you can see
The height and expanse of all there is to be
No more thinking small
Take courage, imagine wide
What a mighty fortress you are
With God on your side!

The grandeur of it all can topple any wall
Like a monumental wave
You are big sky, tall
Push back tiny thoughts
Leave them— buried at sea
Advance yourself. Feast in possibility!

✠ ✠ ✠

CELESTIAL CEILINGS

In the beginning there was something
I didn't know what at that time
So I had to grow up inside myself
I had to observe everybody else's head
See life outside the womb

I poked around, touched some things,
Left others alone
Then, I went by myself to meditate
On what I saw
It was good

I started with nothing. Then the world
Started pulling its enticements onto me
Showed me all the glitters: titles and money
My desire grew to consider this cosmos
The price I had to pay

Was it worth the fall?

Life is not bread alone thrown away
For birds to eat
There is nothing left to prove
I must only improve to show
What is truly valuable

Life is every word I live
Eat, swallow from the heart
I pilgrim the earth by day
Teach me to number them
Well

Let my days give birth like our highborn kinsman
Let me bloom in fields

Leave them pristine
No worldly wind or trendy trends
Mold me

Let me create something equivalent to celestial ceilings
Yes! Sow, when I come home like I was in the beginning
You will be pleased again and whisper,
"Ya done good, earth angel
Ya produced X, Y, and Z"
And I will say,

"That's cause I luv Ya, Daddy!"

✵ ✵ ✵

ACKNOWLEDGEMENTS

I would like to thank so many people for their assistance in making this book happen, but to God be all the praise for giving me the inspiration, motivation, time and talent. To my generous husband who reads and provides commentary on what I write. To my dear family, friends, Denise, Camille, Thelma and Diane who always encourage me in my endeavors.

To Merrill Penalver (I didn't forget you) who edited many of these poems; To all those I forgot to mention by name, I love you too.

Remember: A woman's reach should exceed her grasp, else what's a heaven for.

Ralph Waldo Emerson

ABOUT THE AUTHOR

SE Scott was born in Summerton, South Carolina. She has lived in Florida, and New York.

She now resides in West Orange, New Jersey with her husband, Lynn.

Since retiring as a teacher of English for 30 years, SE has devoted much of her time to writing, media production, community activities, travel, and family.

She also lectures about writing and poetry in schools and other institutions around the country.

SE Scott is co-author of the play A Pearl of a Girl, a coming of age story about five teenage girls.

Although this is SE Scott's first published work, her poems can be viewed on YouTube under the name Mustang2lady. You can email SE at essiece@gmail.com or keepsmilingstandingstrong.wordpress.com

✿ ✿ ✿

www.ingramcontent.com/pod-product-compliance
Lightning Source LLC
Chambersburg PA
CBHW032025090426
42741CB00006B/735